CAUSE AND EFFECT: The Bill of Rights

The Tenth Amendment: States' Rights

BY ELIZABETH RAUM

Consultant:
Richard Bell, PhD
Associate Professor of History
University of Maryland, College Park

CAPSTONE PRESS
a capstone imprint

Fact Finders Books are published by Capstone Press,
1710 Roe Crest Drive, North Mankato, Minnesota 56003
www.mycapstone.com

Copyright © 2018 by Capstone Press, a Capstone imprint. All rights reserved. No part of this publication may be reproduced in whole or in part, or stored in a retrieval system, or transmitted in any form or by any means, electronic, mechanical, photocopying, recording, or otherwise, without written permission of the publisher.

Library of Congress Cataloging-in-Publication Data
Names: Raum, Elizabeth, author.
Title: The Tenth Amendment : states' rights / By Elizabeth Raum.
Description: North Mankato, Minnesota : Capstone Press, 2018. | Series: Fact finders. Cause and effect : the Bill of Rights | Includes bibliographical references and index.
Identifiers: LCCN 2017006676
ISBN 978-1-5157-7162-3 (library binding)
ISBN 978-1-5157-7175-3 (paperback)
ISBN 978-1-5157-7180-7 (eBook PDF)
Subjects: LCSH: United States. Constitution. 10th Amendment—History—Juvenile literature. | States' rights (American politics)—History—Juvenile literature. | Federal government—United States—History—Juvenile literature.
Classification: LCC KF4558 10th .R38 2018 | DDC 342.73/042—dc23
LC record available at https://lccn.loc.gov/2017006676

Editorial Credits
Brenda Haugen, editor; Bobbie Nuytten, designer; Tracey Engel, media researcher; Katy LaVigne, production specialist

Source Notes
Page 18, line 6: James Madison. "The Alleged Danger from the Powers of the Union to the State Governments Considered." Federalist Papers #45. 27 April 2017. https://www.congress.gov/resources/display/content/The+Federalist+Papers#TheFederalistPapers-45
Page 21, line 7: "*McCulloch v. Maryland*, 17 U.S. 316 (1819)," Justia: US Supreme Court. 27 April 2017. https://supreme.justia.com/cases/federal/us/17/316/case.html.
Page 23, sidebar, line 6: "Confederate States of America — Declaration of the Immediate Causes Which Induce and Justify the Secession of South Carolina from the Federal Union." Yale Law School. 24 Dec. 1860. 27 April 2017. http://avalon.law.yale.edu/19th_century/csa_scarsec.asp

Photo Credits
AP Photo, 26; Getty Images: Chicago History Museum, 23, Stock Montage, 15, 21; Library of Congress: http://hdl.loc.gov/locrbc/rbpe.17802600, 6, LC-USZC4-2086, 24 (bottom) LC-DIG-pga-08283, 24 (top); Newscom: Jeff Malet, 10; North Wind Pictures: 7, 22, Gerry Embleton, 12; Shutterstock: Diego G Diaz, 11, Diego Grandi, 20, Everett – Art, 16, Janos Levente, 13 (map background), Joseph Sohm, cover, Kzenon, 4, Rena Schild, 29, Tischenko Irina, cover and interior design element, welcomia, 5, 18
Design Elements: Shutterstock

Printed and bound in the USA.
010399F17

Table of Contents

States in Charge 4
What Caused the Tenth Amendment? 6
Powers to the States 16
Immediate Effects
of the Tenth Amendment 18
Testing the Tenth 20
The Tenth Today 26

Glossary 30
Read More 31
Internet Sites 31
Critical Thinking Questions 32
Index 32

States IN CHARGE

Suppose you want to buy a new bike. The price tag says $100. If you buy it in Rhode Island, you'll have to add a 7 percent state sales tax. Your bike will cost $107. If you buy it in Montana, there's no sales tax. Your bike will cost exactly $100. Why is there a difference in the cost of your bike depending on where you purchase it?

As of 2017, only Alaska, Delaware, Montana, New Hampshire, and Oregon didn't have a statewide sales tax.

Sales taxes are determined by the states. One state may charge a sales tax. Another may not. States issue driver's licenses, **regulate** trade within their borders, and make laws and rules that govern the day-to-day life of their residents. States oversee education and law enforcement within their borders. They establish state police forces and state universities. They maintain state roads and set speed limits. They run state prisons. The state governs many of our everyday activities. The Tenth **Amendment** to the **Constitution** gives them that power.

---

regulate—to make rules that businesses must follow
amendment—a change made to a law or a legal document
Constitution—legal document that describes the basic form of the U.S. government and the rights of citizens
federal—the central government of the United States

FAST FACT:

Powers not granted to the **federal** government are reserved for states and the people.

Each state establishes its own state police force.

WHAT CAUSED the Tenth Amendment?

During the American Revolution (1775–1783), the colonies had formed a loose **confederation**. The country's first constitution, the Articles of Confederation, provided some basic guidelines for the new nation. After the United States won independence, it faced new problems. How would the United States defend its borders? There was no army or navy. What if two states disagreed on an issue? Who was in charge?

The states sent delegates to the Constitutional Convention in Philadelphia, Pennsylvania, in May 1787. The delegates decided to write a new constitution. Some wanted a powerful federal government. Others wanted most of the power to stay with the states. The constitution would determine the future of the country.

confederation—colonies joined together to form a new country

George Washington led the debate at the Constitutional Convention in 1787.

Virginia landowner George Mason wanted to add a bill of rights to the Constitution that would give the people and the states certain rights. A judge and politician, Mason had written Virginia's Bill of Rights. Other states had bills of rights as well. The delegates **debated** Mason's idea for days. In the end, 39 of the 55 delegates voted to approve the Constitution without a bill of rights.

But before the Constitution could take effect, it had to be **ratified** by the state **legislatures**. Many opposed the new Constitution.

Cause #1: Many Leaders Feared a Powerful Central Government

Many **patriot** leaders were against the Constitution. They believed that the Constitution gave too much power to the federal government. They feared that the United States would become like Great Britain. They didn't want a powerful government creating cruel laws or charging unfair taxes. They didn't want a second revolution.

debate—a discussion in which people offer different opinions
ratify—to approve
legislature—the part of government that makes or changes laws
patriot—a person who sided with the colonies during the Revolutionary War

FAST FACT:
Rhode Island refused to send delegates to the Constitutional Convention. Rhode Island's leaders feared they would lose power to the federal government.

Reasons for Missing Signatures

For a variety of reasons, several delegates did not sign the Constitution.

Delegate	State	Reason
Patrick Henry	Virginia	Felt it took away states' rights
George Mason	Virginia	Wanted a bill of rights
Richard Henry Lee	Virginia	Wanted a bill of rights
Edmund Randolph	Virginia	Not enough checks and balances among the three parts of the federal government—the president, Congress, and courts
John Lansing	New York	Opposed to strong federal government
Robert Yates	New York	Opposed to strong federal government
Elbridge Gerry	Massachusetts	Wanted a bill of rights
Caleb Strong	Massachusetts	Opposed to Electoral College, the group that elects the president and vice president after the general election
Luther Martin	Maryland	Felt it took away states' rights
John Mercer	Maryland	Left in protest

Cause #2: The Constitution Seemed to Give Congress Unlimited Powers

Article I, section 8, of the Constitution listed the powers of Congress. The last item gave Congress the power "to make all Laws which shall be necessary and proper for carrying into execution the foregoing Powers." It appeared to many state leaders that Congress could make whatever laws it wanted. State leaders feared that Congress might take away the rights of the people or the powers of the states.

Congress serves as the lawmaking body of the United States.

Powers vs. Rights

The Constitution gives certain *powers* to the government. The Bill of Rights grants certain *rights* to the people. What is the difference? A power is the ability to act as a legal authority. For example, the federal government has the power to declare war. A state has the power to issue driver's licenses and impose sales taxes. A right, on the other hand, is the legal permission to do something or to act in a certain way. Freedom of speech is a right given to the American people by the Bill of Rights. Generally, governments have powers. People have rights.

The right to protest peacefully is granted in the U.S. Bill of Rights.

Cause #3: The States Wanted to Serve the Needs of Their People

Each of the original 13 colonies was unique. The English had settled some areas. The Dutch and Germans had settled in others. People in various colonies spoke different languages. They practiced various customs. Religious beliefs varied from place to place. People did not consider themselves Americans. Their loyalty was to their states, not to their country. They were Virginians or New Yorkers. They believed their state leaders would make decisions serving their needs. They feared that a federal government would not understand their differing needs.

Many Germans settled in Pennsylvania.

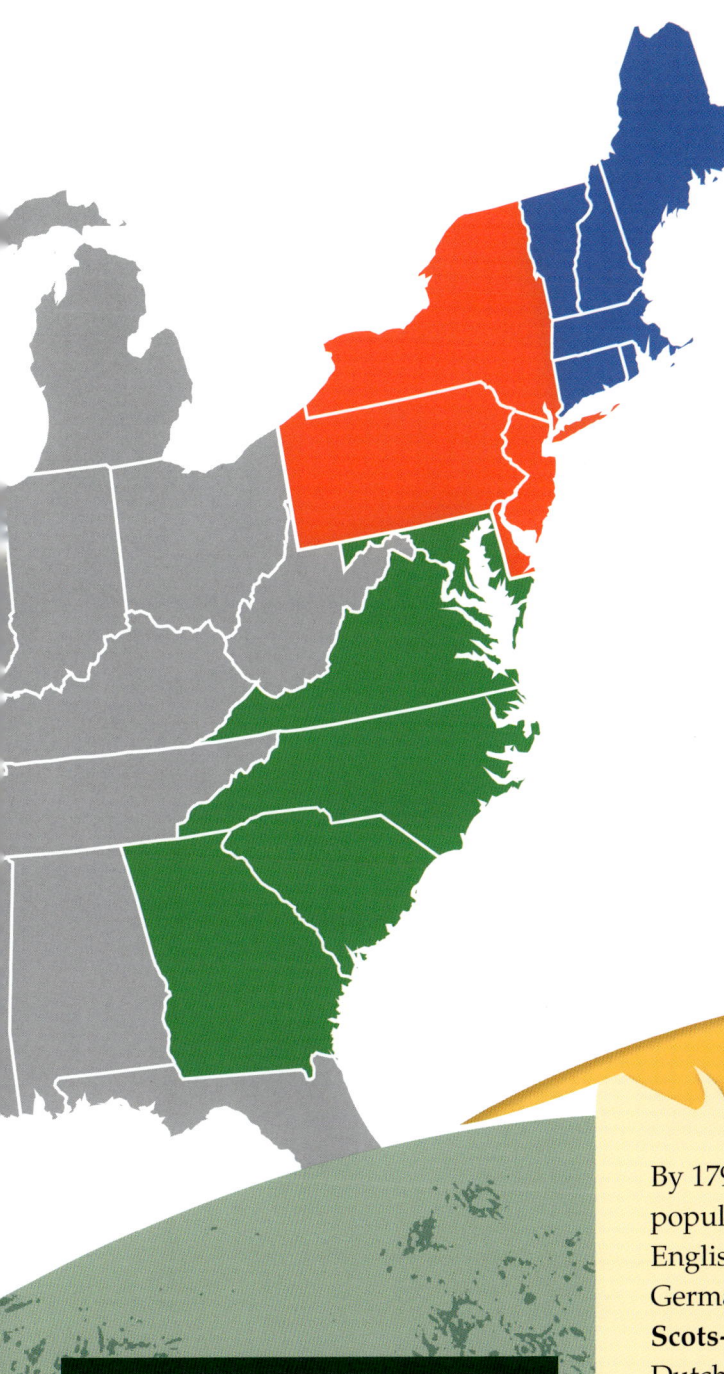

Northern States
Massachusetts
(Maine was part of Massachusetts)
New Hampshire
Vermont
Connecticut
Rhode Island

Middle States
New York
Pennsylvania
New Jersey
Delaware

Southern States
Maryland
Virginia
North Carolina
South Carolina
Georgia

Scots-Irish—people who moved from Scotland to Northern Ireland in the 1600s

FAST FACT:

By 1790, 60 percent of the white population in the United States had English roots. Almost 9 percent were German, 8 percent Scot, 6 percent **Scots-Irish**, 4 percent Irish, and 3 percent Dutch. The rest were Swedish, French, and Spanish. There were also thousands of American Indians and nearly 700,000 African-Americans.

Cause #4: The States Wanted to Control Their Own Economies

The states fell into three regions: northern, middle, and southern. Their geography, climates, and resources varied. As a result they grew different crops and made various products. In the north, for example, fishing and shipbuilding were important. In the south, farmers grew tobacco, rice, and indigo, a blue dye obtained from various plants.

States put **import duties** on goods from other countries. They wanted to keep the import duties. They didn't want the federal government to take them away.

Cause #5: Southern States Feared that Congress Would Vote to End Slavery

Twenty-five of the 55 delegates to the Constitutional Convention were slave owners. Even so, many of the delegates were against slavery. Several northern states also opposed it, though slavery was legal in every state except Massachusetts and New Hampshire.

The Constitution didn't mention slavery, but southerners feared the northern states would create laws against it. Many southern farmers depended on slave labor. John Rutledge of South Carolina insisted that slavery should be controlled by the states.

import duty—a tax placed on goods coming from another country

Men loaded barrels of tobacco onto ships in the James River in Virginia in the 1700s.

Trade interests of the original states in the 1700s

Northern States	Middle States	Southern States
Fish	Wheat	Tobacco
Shipbuilding	Corn	Rice
Lumber	Lumber	Lumber
Iron	Iron	Iron
	Dairy products	Indigo
	Rye	Furs
	Furs	

Powers TO THE STATES

When the Constitution went to the states for approval, many thought of the words of the Declaration of Independence: "… these United Colonies are, and of Right ought to be Free and Independent States." The Constitution seemed to take away at least some of that independence.

Anti-Federalist leaders such as Patrick Henry of Virginia and Samuel Adams of Massachusetts opposed ratification. After much debate, Rhode Island, Massachusetts, New Hampshire, Virginia, and New York ratified the Constitution. They also included strong recommendations that a bill of rights be added. In fact, it seemed to be a condition of their votes. The North Carolina legislature also asked that a "declaration of rights" be presented to Congress.

James Madison of Virginia introduced a federal bill of rights to the First Congress in 1789. His Bill of Rights became the first 10 amendments to the Constitution. The Tenth Amendment granted certain powers to the states.

James Madison

anti-Federalist—a person who was against a strong central government and wanted states' rights included in the U.S. Constitution

The Bill of Rights

Amendment I
Congress shall make no law respecting an establishment of religion, or prohibiting the free exercise thereof; or abridging the freedom of speech, or of the press; or the right of the people peaceably to assemble, and to petition the government for a redress of grievances.

Amendment II
A well regulated militia, being necessary to the security of a free state, the right of the people to keep and bear arms, shall not be infringed.

Amendment III
No soldier shall, in time of peace be quartered in any house, without the consent of the owner, nor in time of war, but in a manner to be prescribed by law.

Amendment IV
The right of the people to be secure in their persons, houses, papers, and effects, against unreasonable searches and seizures, shall not be violated, and no warrants shall issue, but upon probable cause, supported by oath or affirmation, and particularly describing the place to be searched, and the persons or things to be seized.

Amendment V
No person shall be held to answer for a capital, or otherwise infamous crime, unless on a presentment or indictment of a grand jury, except in cases arising in the land or naval forces, or in the militia, when in actual service in time of war or public danger; nor shall any person be subject for the same offense to be twice put in jeopardy of life or limb; nor shall be compelled in any criminal case to be a witness against himself, nor be deprived of life, liberty, or property, without due process of law; nor shall private property be taken for public use, without just compensation.

Amendment VI
In all criminal prosecutions, the accused shall enjoy the right to a speedy and public trial, by an impartial jury of the state and district wherein the crime shall have been committed, which district shall have been previously ascertained by law, and to be informed of the nature and cause of the accusation; to be confronted with the witnesses against him; to have compulsory process for obtaining witnesses in his favor, and to have the assistance of counsel for his defense.

Amendment VII
In suits at common law, where the value in controversy shall exceed twenty dollars, the right of trial by jury shall be preserved, and no fact tried by a jury, shall be otherwise reexamined in any court of the United States, than according to the rules of the common law.

Amendment VIII
Excessive bail shall not be required, nor excessive fines imposed, nor cruel and unusual punishments inflicted.

Amendment IX
The enumeration in the Constitution, of certain rights, shall not be construed to deny or disparage others retained by the people.

Amendment X
The powers not delegated to the United States by the Constitution, nor prohibited by it to the states, are reserved to the states respectively, or to the people.

IMMEDIATE EFFECTS
of the Tenth Amendment

The Tenth Amendment granted certain powers to the states. Some effects were clear right away.

Effect #1: Emphasized Limited Power of the Federal Government

The Tenth Amendment reassured people that the federal government's powers were limited to those stated in the Constitution. In 1788 James Madison wrote a message "To the People of the State of New York." In it he said, "The powers delegated by the proposed Constitution to the Federal Government are few and defined. Those which are to remain in the State Governments are numerous and indefinite." The Tenth Amendment supported the idea that the federal government did not have unlimited power.

Effect #2: Reassured the States that They Could Keep Their Powers

The Tenth Amendment guaranteed powers to each of the states to make laws that directly affect activities within the state. States can establish local governments, conduct elections, issue licenses, and control trade within the state. States can impose taxes needed to pay for various activities, such as education, public health, and road building.

Who's in Charge?

While some powers rest with only the federal or state governments, some are shared between the two.

Powers of the federal government

Declare war

Print money

Establish an army and navy

Enter into treaties with foreign governments

Control trade between states and other nations

Make laws necessary to enforce the Constitution

Establish post offices and issue postage

Powers of the state governments

Establish local governments

Issue licenses (driver's, hunting, marriage, etc.)

Conduct elections

Provide for the public health and safety

Control trade within the state

Ratify amendments to the Constitution

Exercise powers not given to the federal government

Shared powers

Set up courts

Create and collect taxes

Build highways

Make and enforce laws

Charter banks and corporations

Spend money for the general welfare

Borrow money

Take private property for public purposes, with just **compensation**

---

compensation—payment or reward

TESTING *the Tenth*

Over the years, the Tenth Amendment has been tested in the courts. The Supreme Court has the power to overturn state laws that violate the Constitution. This is called **judicial review**.

One of the most important tests was the case of *McCulloch v. Maryland*. Congress established the Second Bank of the United States in 1816. Two years later the state of Maryland taxed the bank. James McCulloch, the bank's cashier, refused to pay. Did Congress have the right to establish a bank? Did Maryland have the power to tax it?

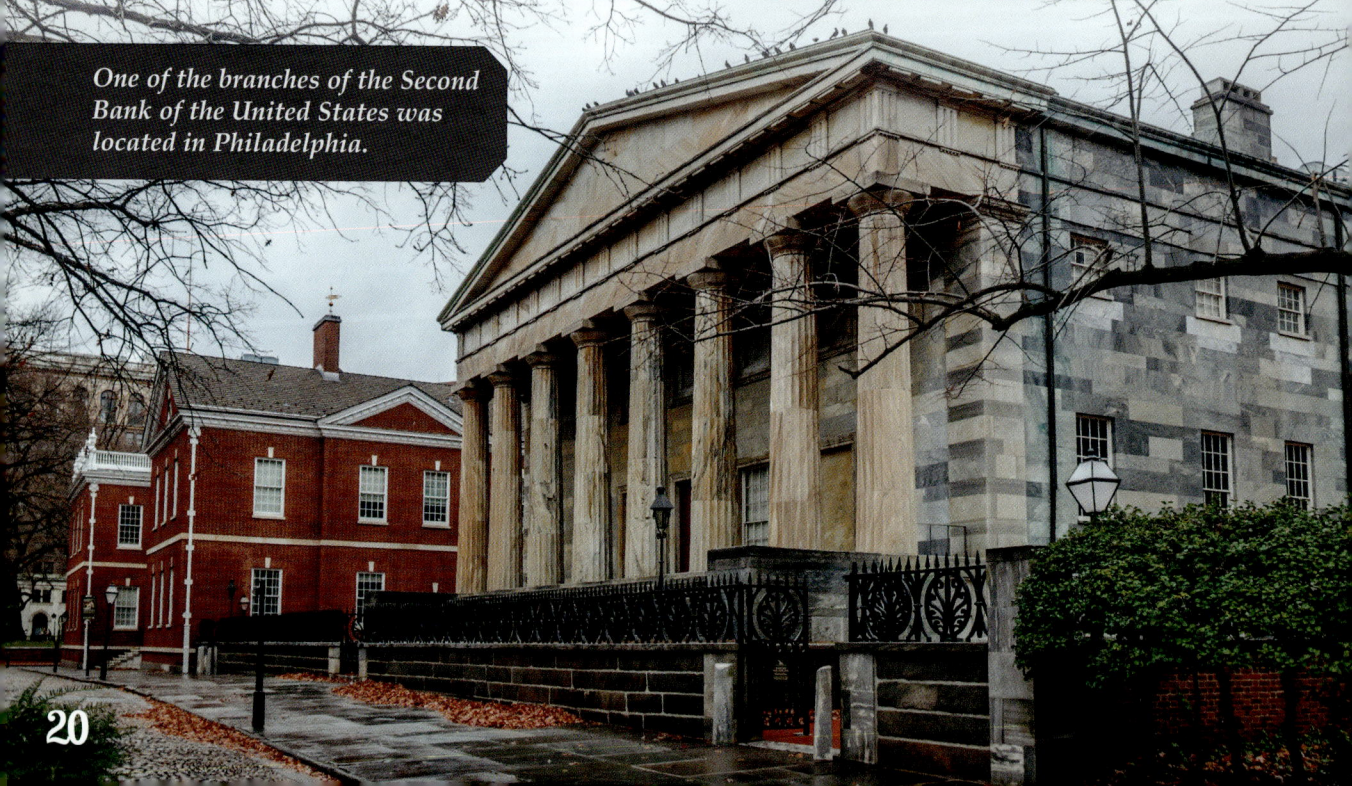

One of the branches of the Second Bank of the United States was located in Philadelphia.

The Supreme Court ruled against Maryland. Chief Justice John Marshall cited Article 1, Section 8, of the Constitution. It gives Congress the power "to make all Laws which shall be necessary and proper…." Congress has the power to collect taxes and borrow money. The bank helped Congress do that.

Maryland could not tax the bank. Marshall wrote, "The power to tax involves the power to destroy." The state does not have the power to tax the federal government. The **Supremacy** Clause of the Constitution says that federal law overrules state law.

> **judicial review**—the power of the court to determine if a law or act goes against the Constitution
> **supremacy**—having the last or final power or authority

Shaping the Nation

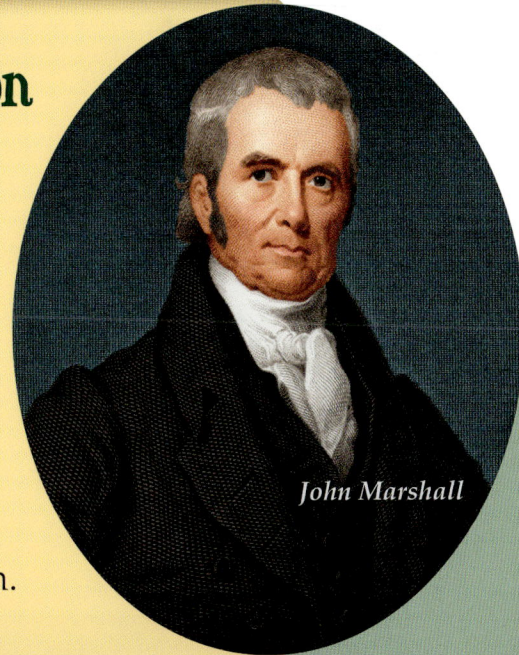
John Marshall

John Marshall (1755–1835) of Virginia was the fourth chief justice of the Supreme Court. His decisions helped to establish the role of the Supreme Court and to defend the role of the federal government. He ruled in more than 1,000 cases. Many, such as *McCulloch v. Maryland*, helped shaped the young nation.

The issue of slavery tested the Tenth Amendment again. The southern states had feared that the North would attempt to ban slavery. That didn't happen, but many in the North refused to follow a federal law called the Fugitive Slave Act. Congress passed the Fugitive Slave Act in 1850. It required states to return escaped slaves. Many northern states refused. They ignored a federal law. Instead, the northern states created personal-liberty laws to protect escaped slaves.

During the next 10 years, tensions increased between slave owners and **abolitionists**. On December 20, 1860, South Carolina **seceded** from the United States. South Carolina's leaders wrote that the refusal of the North to obey federal laws violated the Constitution. After all, the Supremacy Clause put federal laws above those of any state.

Slave hunters sometimes used dogs to track down fugitive slaves.

South Carolina Makes a Statement

On December 24, 1860, South Carolina issued a "Declaration of the Immediate Causes Which Induce and Justify the Secession of South Carolina from the Federal Union." It said:

"We, therefore, the People of South Carolina … have solemnly declared that the Union … between this State and the other States of North America, is dissolved, and that the State of South Carolina has resumed her position among the nations of the world, as a separate and independent State; with full power to levy war, conclude peace, contract alliances, establish **commerce**, and to do all other acts and things which independent States may of right do."

---

abolitionist—a person who worked to end slavery before the Civil War
secede—to withdraw from
commerce—the exchange of goods, often between states or countries

Ten more states followed South Carolina's lead. They formed the Confederate States of America. These states claimed that it was their right as free and independent states to secede from the Union. President Abraham Lincoln and the northern states disagreed. They viewed secession as illegal. They went to war.

The Civil War (1861–1865) lasted for four years. About 750,000 men died in the war. At war's end, the South rejoined the Union. Lincoln freed the slaves, and Congress passed the Fourteenth Amendment. The Fourteenth Amendment made it illegal for states to deny anyone "life, liberty, or property." Former slaves were now citizens.

Abraham Lincoln

the Battle of Corinth, Mississippi, October 4, 1862

Since that time, the Supreme Court has cited the Fourteenth Amendment in hundreds of cases. It supports the rights of individuals, and when states' rights come into conflict with individual rights, the people win.

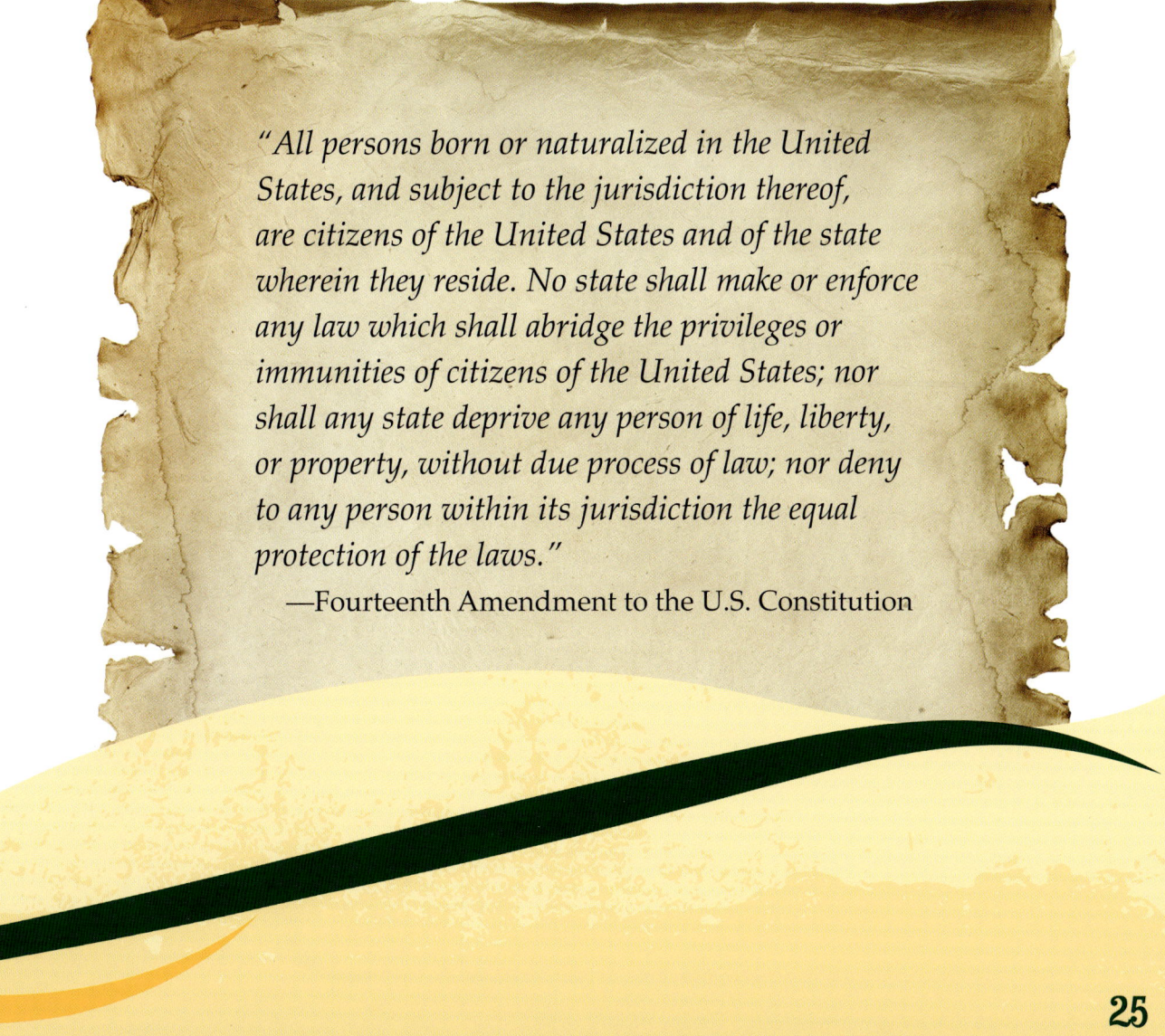

"All persons born or naturalized in the United States, and subject to the jurisdiction thereof, are citizens of the United States and of the state wherein they reside. No state shall make or enforce any law which shall abridge the privileges or immunities of citizens of the United States; nor shall any state deprive any person of life, liberty, or property, without due process of law; nor deny to any person within its jurisdiction the equal protection of the laws."
—Fourteenth Amendment to the U.S. Constitution

The Tenth TODAY

Challenges to the Tenth Amendment did not end with the Civil War. They continue today. Some people believe the federal government has taken power that belongs to the states. Others believe the Supreme Court has made good decisions, especially in protecting the people's rights, even if it means overturning state laws. What do you think?

Brown v. Board of Education

The Supreme Court ruled on *Brown v. Board of Education* in 1954. In this case, laws in several states required black children and white children to attend separate but equal schools. The Supreme Court ruled that "separate but equal" schools were **unconstitutional**. The court cited the Fourteenth Amendment in its decision. Most laws regarding education belong to the states, but in this case, the rights of the individual outweighed the laws of the states.

George E.C. Hayes, Thurgood Marshall (center), and James M. Nabrit were the lawyers who fought for the end of "separate but equal" schools.

United States v. Lopez

The Gun-Free School Zones Act of 1990 made it a federal crime to carry a gun into a school. In 1995 high school senior Alfonzo Lopez brought a gun to school. He was arrested for breaking a Texas law. Federal lawyers took over. They charged Lopez with a federal crime. Who was in charge?

The Supreme Court ruled in favor of the state. The Court decided the Gun-Free School Zone Act was unconstitutional. Under the U.S. Constitution, gun laws belong to the state. However, the federal government controls interstate commerce, so cases involving transporting guns across state borders are a federal issue.

unconstitutional—not in agreement with the Constitution

Shelby County v. Holder

Section 4 of the Voting Rights Act of 1965 required certain southern states to get federal approval before changing their voting laws. It was an effort to fight **discrimination**. Shelby County, Alabama, brought the case to the Supreme Court. There was no evidence of voter discrimination in Shelby County, but the county had to obey the law. The Supreme Court ruled that the law was unconstitutional. The power to conduct elections belongs to the states.

Obergefell v. Hodges

In June 2015 the Supreme Court ruled that same-sex marriage is legal in all 50 states. Before the ruling, 37 states allowed same-sex marriage, while 13 did not. The court cited the Fourteenth Amendment and said that the right to marry is protected by the Constitution. Before the ruling, marriage laws had been left to the states. That is no longer true.

> **discrimination**—unfair treatment of a person or group, often because of race, religion, gender, sexual orientation, or age

More Issues to Come

Some people want to expand the power of the federal government. The states now make laws about hate speech, gun control, marijuana use, insurance, and end-of-life issues. Should the federal government get involved? Watch for more Supreme Court cases concerning the Tenth Amendment.

A crowd gathered outside the Supreme Court after its 2015 ruling on same-sex marriage.

GLOSSARY

abolitionist (ab-uh-LI-shuhn-ist)—a person who worked to end slavery before the Civil War

amendment (uh-MEND-muhnt)—a change made to a law or a legal document

anti-Federalist (AN-tye-fed-ur-uhl-ist)—a person who was against a strong central government and wanted states' rights included in the U.S. Constitution

commerce (KAH-murss)—the exchange of goods, often between states or countries

compensation (kahm-pen-SAY-shuhn)—payment or reward

confederation (kuhn-fed-dur-AY-shuhn)—colonies joined together to form a new country

constitution (kahn-stuh-TOO-shuhn)—legal document that describes the basic form of the U.S. government and the rights of citizens

debate (di-BAYT)—a discussion in which people offer different opinions

discrimination (dis-kri-muh-NAY-shuhn)—unfair treatment of a person or group, often because of race, religion, gender, sexual orientation, or age

federal (FED-ur-uhl)—the central government of the United States

import duty (IM-port DOO-tee)—a tax placed on goods coming from another country

judicial review (joo-DISH-uh ri-VYOO)—the power of the court to determine if a law or act goes against the Constitution

legislature (LEJ-iss-lay-chur)—the part of government that makes or changes laws

patriot (PAY-tree-uht)—a person who sided with the colonies during the Revolutionary War

ratify (RAH-tuh-fye)—to approve

regulate (REG-yuh-layt)—to make rules that businesses must follow

Scots-Irish (SKOTS-EYE-rish)—people who moved from Scotland to Northern Ireland in the 1600s

secede (si-SEED)—to withdraw from

supremacy (soo-PREM-uh-see)—having the last or final power or authority

unconstitutional (un-kon-stuh-TOO-shuhn-uhl)—not in agreement with the Constitution

READ MORE

Baxter, Roberta. *The Bill of Rights.* Chicago: Heinemann Library, 2013.

Krull, Kathleen. *A Kid's Guide to America's Bill of Rights.* New York: Harper, 2015.

Spier, Peter. *We the People: The Constitution of the United States.* New York: Doubleday, 2014.

INTERNET SITES

Use FactHound to find Internet sites related to this book.

Visit *www.facthound.com*

Just type in 9781515771623 and go.

 Check out projects, games and lots more at www.capstonekids.com

CRITICAL THINKING QUESTIONS

1. Using details from the text, describe how the Tenth Amendment served to support the interests of the states.
2. How does the chart on page 19 help clarify the Tenth Amendment?
3. How would the United States be different if it did not have a strong federal government and governing was left entirely to the states?

INDEX

Adams, Samuel, 16
American Revolution, 6

Civil War, 24, 26

education, 5, 18, 26

Fourteenth Amendment, 24–25, 28

Gun-Free School Zones Act, 27

Henry, Patrick, 16

import duties, 14

law enforcement, 5
Lincoln, Abraham, 24
Lopez, Alfonzo, 27

Madison, James, 16, 18
Marshall, John, 21
Mason, George, 8
McCulloch, James, 20

prisons, 5

Rutledge, John, 14

sales taxes, 4–5, 11
same-sex marriage, 28
slavery, 14, 22
speed limits, 5
Supremacy Clause, 21, 22

trade, 5, 18

Voting Rights Act, 28